JET-SETTER

JET-SETTER

Handbook for Flying

Thomas Mhlaba

To order additional copies of this book, contact:
Xlibris LLC
1-888-795-4274
www.Xlibris.com
Orders@Xlibris.com
551471

CONTENTS

Dedications

I would like to thank my wife Vee for encouraging me to write and believing in me. Many thanks to my kids Craig and Hailey for inspiring me and giving me a purpose to survive. Stakes of gratitude to my parents for making me the man I am today. A big hug to my siblings for being there always especially my sisters Angie and Dee and my aunt Lizzy. Chris and M'Colly, you know how it is boys. To my late brother Man Raving Gansol, may he Rest in Peace.

Above all let me take this opportunity to thank The Man Above for giving me the will to persevere, the hunger to hunt for success. The courage to conquer new grounds and the decency to stay humble in the process. May your wish be granted and let the North star shine upon us so that mankind knows your greatness. I BELIEVE

INTRODUCTION

It is a fact that every Tom, Dick and Harry dream of finding their cute behinds glued to the seats of a Boeing, Airbus or any other crapy aircraft that their not so deep pockets' can afford to fly on. Whatever tinkles your fancy or tickles your pocket, here are some hot tips that will make you enjoy or spoil your experience.

Listen,I don't care who you are or where you are from. You might be Royalty or a super slave. All you have to do right now is to trust me because I am the only 'Sensei' of the subject that I am about to preach. I apologies in advance for my arrogance, that's if you think I am. In actual fact, I am not. All I need from you is to understand one simple thing that I always feel my warm blood flow in my veins with excitement when I preach of my specialty. I get a blend of excitement and pride when I talk about my experience. Do not blame me when my lingo becomes flowery when I preach, for I adopted flamboyancy from a peacock. Enough about me, let's revert to the subject.

For a zillion years mankind have lived on theories. Theories, principles whatever you wanna call them have seen a lot of people go far in there careers, communities, societies, nations and some globally. These theories can not be disputed 'loudly' because mankind will think one has lost respect for those that have departed. But there is one aspect that I know for a fact that you know jack sh*t about,'FLYING'.

I know it took some individuals centuries to save for their first and obviously their last flight, and a fraction of a second for a few clever ones who swindled piles of notes from the rich that didn't see it coming. And I know for a fact that some of you had to kiss butt so as to have a chance to become jet-setters. Whichever means or ways you used to make yourself one (jet-setter) really doesn't concern me. All you have to do is thank whoever you pray to for making you live your dream.

As a good parent let me take this opportunity to mother you before you go out there and embarrass yourself. I understand you are on top of the moon now as you are about to live your dream, but please don't get carried away and start jumping from one branch to another like a monkey. Don't lose your marbles yet. Hold it 'china'. Everything that you assumed you knew about flying is about to change. All your theories and beliefs are about to be proven wrong. Hey, why do you suddenly look confused and afraid? I can see you are trying to present a brave face. Please don't, I can smell your fear from here. Ok heads up soldier. Don't be scared. This book you are going through right now will guide you through the do's and don'ts of a jet-setter. Seat back, relax and let the supper jet-setter guide you through.

GETTING TO THE AIRPORT

It is guaranteed that I will hold you responsible for getting lost for a straight hour trying to get to the departures terminal of any airport. Ok let me be nice, I understand you don't stay at the airport. Check. The last time you visited one was when you were a pupil on a school trip. It's ok I understand. I don't blame you, I blame your poor dad who couldn't afford to get you on a plane. If you were clever or had a choice, you could have chosen a cool dad like what my little man Craig and rowdy Hailey did. They hand picked the coolest jet-setter dad who made sure that they got to understand the term 'travel in style' at a tender age. Viva Craig, viva Hailey! You make me proud. Some cool choice you made. Enough about these brats. My little heroes.

CHECKING IN

On a lighter note, I will not hold you accountable if you find yourself screaming and shouting at the agents at the check-in counters, airport security, baggage handlers or any other ground personnel before you set foot on a jet. These people are renowned of hate and jealousy. All they do is upset you before your wonderful experience. Oh yeah you heard me, 'wonderful experience'.

One thing for a fact, check in agents don't really pay attention to what you say to them. All they worry about is to quickly close the flights and try catch shebeens (unlicensed drinking spot) before they close. If you don't believe me, ask yourself why they keep on repeating the same stupid questions whilst they have your ticket in their hands that has all the information they need to know. For example, they always ask your name, destination, which airline you flying on and at times they even ask if you are flying alone of which even if you not the system only reflects an individual per ticket unless if it was a group booking. Anyway, enough of their stupidity. Guess they attendant night school, all they have to do is to adjust airport lights to dim maybe they can become effective.

SECURITY CHECKS

When it comes to security checks don't even waste your breath. Security people only want to take your drinks and food for personal consumption. So one hot tip from the jet-setter if you are carrying alcohol and they try to confiscate it simply because its more than 100 ml in quantity. All you have to do is step aside and open,'that' drink of your choice and drain it down your throat with pride. Even if you don't have a dash for it, just gulp it like a man. I know you can do it. If its food, spit on it, rub it under your armpits, wipe your ass with it. Do everything nasty that comes to your mind 'china' but if they stop you, please comply or else you will be booted out of the building. It's not definite though. For heavens sake you have a right to do as you please. After all it is your stash homeboy.

If they want to do a body search on you, I edge you to comply. Maybe they suspect you of smuggling some illegal substance or you are simply a hunk and these whores cant resists your muscular figure. If you are a 'she', know that same sh*t is happening to you. Anyway if they succeed to strip you and your belongings apart, just keep your cool. Whatever you do, please do not lose it because these guys can stop you from living your dream. All you can do is bitch and moan whilst co-operating. Let your mouth do the opposite of your action. If you do this, know you are close to your experience.

When these bimbos are done strip searching you and your belongings please proceed with ambiance to your respective boarding gate. Even though check in agents and security personnel have tried to spoil the first minutes of your dream, don't let it affect your awareness or you will find yourself at a wrong boarding gate. If you are really upset this is your chance to calm down your nerves. As you walk into an airport, any airport worldwide all you have to do is keep your eyes wide open. There is always a drinking spot. Find one and drown your sorrows, but be warned the drinks are charged at hotel price. Why should I be worried? You are a jet-setter. Whatever you decide please make sure you set an alarm or else you will miss your flight. Oh yah one other thing, please don't drink too much or else you will not be allowed aboard an aircraft. Remember this is a state of the art machine not a drunk mans' roller coaster. You have been warned.

BOARDING

As you walk towards an aircraft try to relax as much as possible but don't be too casual, people around you might think you are lost. If you are American be warned not to ask if one is African and frown if you see them wearing shoes. Do not ask if you gonna see lions on landing because The Motherland isn't a massive game-park. But if you insist on asking, go ahead and chances are you might just make a day of your fellow travelers by your unique ignorance. No offense intended you guys are just experts when it comes to ignorance. Since this world was declared a global village most of you assume that all Africans are literally neighbors. Check this out,

"Excuse me, do u you know John he is a good friend of mine he stays in Angola, tell him I said hello".

Hello! Damn ass, I live in Johannesburg. Anyway I can't blame you. How many of you have passports? Chances are

Bush never had one till the time he was voted into the White house. Please don't take it personal, it's just my opinion. Moving forward.

When you step aboard a jet always show a boarding pass to the flight attendant at the door. If you want to play rich do not greet this person in your face. Just look straight in his/her eyes and node slightly. I promise you the attendant will greet you first. Make your response is abrupt but friendly. Listen to me, don't be too friendly and ask the attendants about their personal being. They (flight attendant) will obviously know that you are going to be a pain in the butt. If it's a lady at your service please avoid flirting, it won't take you anyway. All you will be asking for is a middle name like pig, cow, etc. You catch my drift. Unless if you are extremely handsome then you can try your luck. Food for thought, imagine how many wanna be's try their ancient pick up lines on these gorgeous hostesses daily. Now you understand.

As an American again, please don't come with your 'foot foot' nonsense of back ache, or 'I just got out of surgery for an operation and the doctor advised you to have maximum comfort on the plane' story. Trust me the flight crew have heard it all. If you really need rest don't you think it is wise to stay home till you fully recovered. Also don't try to take your chances by lying that the guys at the check in counters promised you that the crew will upgrade once you are aboard. That line won't work, the guys at the counters have the powers to upgrade not the flight crew. And if you are on a honey moon please avoid embarrassing yourself by trying to gamble for a business class seat either. If you were able to marry her then you should be able to afford a business class seat for your bride. But if you can't afford one, you must try bringing some presents for the crew maybe you might get something out of them. Obviously not an upgrade but maybe a bottle of Champagne from the elite class. Did I say Champagne, I am so sorry I almost mislead you. I meant sparkling wine. If you don't know the difference I suggest you google it.

If you think you are popular. For example a hip hop artist, an actor, a sports man, a drama queen or a kwaito (South African hip hop) star please do not expect hugs and kisses. Flight crew is as famous as you are. Ok maybe not famous, but popular. Do not ask if they don't know who you are, especially if you have some sort of 'unique' name like Doctor or Mercedes. They will assume you are bragging about your profession or car. Don't get me wrong, these guys are no dumb asses. They just like playing mind games, oh yeah and some other games too. You feel me?

If you are a politician you can take your chances but be warned, success is not guaranteed. You might be playing for the wrong team. If you are a BEE (Black Empowered Entity) please just go to your seat and zip it or you will annoy the person at your service by talking about you million dollar deals. Don't get me wrong these guys don't hate rich people, all there are against is rich people showing off their wealth. Remember money in your bank account doesn't do much for the hostess at your service. Fact!

If you are a Nun or Man of God (Priest) you can do whatever you want and get away with it. Guaranteed. Crew is religious and it's a fact that ninety-nine percent carry Bibles, Holy Quran and/ the book of Mammon.

Although I understand that you are a religious man please avoid asking the crew which direction is north during the flight when you want to show off your praying skills. Chances are they (crew) will point at any direction and laugh at you when you tie your arms tight with some duck tape and put on a torch with flat batteries on your forehead and speak in tongues whiles you bend down ass stuck up in the air and hum some harmonious rhythm before lifting your head up in prayer. Anyway it is not a train smash. Why worry, you are a jet-setter.

AFTER BOARDING

When you get to your seat stow away your bags. Please don't ask the poor steward or stewardess to stow them away for you. There are not there for baggage management. You pack it, you rack it. Damn right you heard me, 'pack it rack it'. And whilst you at it please be prompt. You might be blocking the flow of traffic on the plane. Be as spontaneous as possible. Always make sure that you're aware of your surroundings. Try to find your seat as quickly as possible. As soon as you find it, please glue your cute behind into it and let the traffic flow. Never stand in the isle for long pretending to be looking for space to shove your bag in, or take off your jacket from Shenzhen (China) and stuff it in the stowage whilst other customers are behind you admiring a not so appetizing strip show of yours. It's just selfish and childish. Anyway who knows, maybe you didn't get much attention during your childhood.

When you are comfortable in your seat you can fiddle with your mobile phone, make a call or just seat back and await the actual moment of truth. Don't don the headset provided as yet. The entertainment system is normally off before take off. If it is a domestic flight don't even bother looking or asking for them (headphones). Most airlines don't have time to entertain short term jet-setters. Just kidding. Proceeding. Remember this is not the time to show off your gadgets as well. Keep them locked in your cabin bag or else the crew will make you switch them off. If they do, don't take it personal, or think they are picking on you or they are jealousy. No not all, they are just calling you to order. Besides these guys (flight attendants) have more gadgets than you have. Imagine how many times they have visited China. Now you see, clearly you can't beat them. They have the most recent crap that the technology world has to offer. Again if you are American, 'SORRY AMERICANS but please don't embarrass yourself by telling these guys that whatever you have in your hands is not a phone but an I-phone. Same crap, trust me. Also like mentioned earlier on, these guys are not dumb. So don't put your phone on standby and try to fool them into believing that your phone is off or else you will get a crash course on how to switch your phone off. Enough about flight crew.

Also if you are thirsty or hungry please don't ask for water or food at this point in time. You should have bought yourself some as you walked through the airport building. So you understand never to make your problems other peoples'. That's why your mother always packed lunch for you when you went to school. Think ahead Charlie, think ahead.

When boarding is complete pay attention to the safety video. The stuff they show shall become handy and save your cute butt when the need arises, but be warned. DO NOT, I repeat Do NOT laugh when they do manual safety demonstrations, popularly known as the 'puppet show'. All you will be doing is crushing these guys (crew) egos. That's if you will be able to succeed.

If you are sitting at an emergency exit and you are black African please don't blow your own horns by telling crew that you don't want to have people's lives in your hands. Who said you gonna fly the aircraft? All you are being asked for is to open the damn door in an emergency. In actual fact you are being offered an opportunity to get out of the plane first if sh*t hits the fan. Another thing, if you do not speak or understand English and the flight crew decides to move you to another seat please do not take it personal. Its just a safety issue. Imagine if a simple command like 'EVACUATE' don't mean a thing to you.

If you have blankets provided for the flight and the cabin crew take them away from you prior to take off, please comply. It's a sensible thing to do. Imagine having a dispute with your GP. Remember this person is a trained professional. Think of it, you suggesting medication to him simply because you are assuming or you think you know what you are suffering from.

If you are feeling cold do not blame the aircraft just check which side of earth you are from. If you are from India or Senegal then blame it on your home weather. Anyway blankets may hinder a safe and quick evacuation, thus if the need arises. I don't want you to fall face down when you trip and fall from your own covers. Now you understand. Thank you.

Whatever the crew ask you to do you must comply. Cut the crap and stop arguing and try to justify the situation at hand with your previous experiences. The truth is no-one wants to share your memories. They are yours so keep them to yourself and cherish them.

After all the jazz, seat back relax and await for the magic. Oh yeah make sure your seatbelt is fastened at all times. You hear me, at all times ok. I just don't wanna see you tossing up and down like cheap pop corn at a movie house when you hit turbulence. You follow? After all I care.

TAKE OFF

Take off is magical and super fascinating, but if it's your first one please hold your bowels. I don't want to see you spoil your garb as the state of the machine is blasted to full power for an amazing lift. Hold one homeboy the moment of truth has arrived. You are about to get airborne. Just remember most accidents in the history of aviation happen during this phase of the flight and on approach. Just some juicy information that the jet-setter has to share with you. Hold it China, I am not trying to scare you. I m sharing vital information, but trust me if you are flying with one of the best and safest airliners in the world you are definitely going to be all right. The 'adidas boys' (Pilots) on controls where trained by the military. Yeah most of them, so if they survived flying in combat this is a piece of pie for them. Look out through the window and see how fast the airport building is flying in opposite direction. Listen to the roar of the Rolls Royce engines powering your thrust and conquering gravity. Can you feel it? Thats what I am talking about folks, right there is the moment of magic jet-setter. Ugh yeah!

CRUISE PHASE

After take off do not try to rush to the toilet before the seat-belts sign go off. You have to learn to hold it, period. Unless if you are Chinese then you can play the 'NO ENGLISH' card. At this moment, try not to switch on the entertainment system as yet, it's still off. Remember to relax and let the super jet-setter take care of you. Always remember wise man's words, "good things come to those who wait". Patience homeboy. As soon as you have taken off you will definitely hear a voice over the PA of a glorified jet-setter welcoming you to the skies and informing you about the services on board to spice up your experience. After that voice another one in control takes over and shower you with the technical side of your trip. The voice will tell you about the wind speed, the direction you took off, the height above sea level you are cruising at and all the fancy stuff. Don't be fooled, he is jus a glorified bus driver in charge of this beautiful baby. You didn't hear it from me. Soon 'FASTEN SEAT BELTS LIGHTS' will go off and if you really wanted to go to the loo now is your chance. If you are traveling in the elite class on an Airbus brace yourself because you are about to experience a toilet with a view. Please don't forget to take your camera with, you will definitely need evidence when you land because your homies will not believe you. So the guy who wrote or spoke about a toilet with a view is not a genius he just flew and observed. Kak (Afrikaans for defecate) in style my man. After your relief moment please always flush. Don't leave the toilet with your stuff full in the pot. Even if it's your first time on a plane, please look for a button or lever to make sure that your mess is gone. Do not I repeat do not try to cover it up with toilet paper, its just not right. You have been begged jet-setter. If the reason for your visit to the loo was to puke please do it in the pot as well not the basin unless you do that at your home then I won't hold any wrongdoing against you. Back to your sit now.

A few minutes from this point, the feast begins. When drinks are being served, wait for your turn. Do not jump the gun. When your turn comes avoid ordering for your hubby or wifey, unless they are dumb. I know its a bit embarrassing to ask especially if you don't know whats on the beverage list but please don't be shy, do ask always or else you will be stuck with some drink that has a fancy name but tastes like sh*t. Always order for your kids. These little brats must not be given a chance to choose for themselves. They annoy the day light out of crew members. I am sorry I have to teach you how to raise your brats/

bastards, if I don't who will? There is no time to entertain these little annoying 'things' period. Oh in case you are wandering, I do have two beautiful kids. Remember Hailey and Craig?

Always try to be classy and order some descent quantity. You never know, some airlines charge for beverages but if you're flying Africa's best airline then you can go ahead and spoil yourself. But remember if you order too much booze the crew will know that you either Afrikaans or Indian from Durban. (South Africa's east coast city). If you are black they will assume you are from Tembisa (Johannesburg's Northern black township). If you are not only black but with a funny accent, they will definitely know you are Nigerian. But not a 'train smash' only your position on the personal status log will suffer but your jet-setter status won't be affected. Anyway, why worry you are already living your dream.

When these guys return with a meal cart listen carefully. They normally ask a tricky question. CHICKEN or BEEF? Once again don't be caught shouting with your headset on or taking off reading glasses trying to figure out the magic answer. Chances are you will irritate the day light out of the attendant serving you. With headphones on you are bound to scream, FISH! What can I say? You are a jet-setter. Remember you have been warned.

Also this is not the time to ask for a second drink. The crew only have solid food for you. The drinks cart is securely docked in the galley (aircraft kitchen). Besides you have been offered a chance to get a second drink for your meal and you confirmed you were ok. So please stay ok till the drinks come again.

If you don't get your meal choice, please do not scream or swear at the person serving you. Remember all he or she does is serve you, not cook the meal. Unless if you are brave and you want to hear them (crew) suggesting to jump out of the plane and go fishing for you. Damn right, you heard me. Don't ever try to shoot the messenger, it's not fulfilling. It just a waste of time, unless if u have a lot of it (time) on your hands.

When eating whilst watching a movie or listening to some slow jams, always make sure you pause whatever you are busy with and pay attention to the flight attendants when they talk to you. Arrogance will not make you a glorified jet-setter but a hungry traveller. These guys will not worry about your stomach. If you want their attention, do not make hissing sounds like a snake or flip your fingers like a street dice player. No-one will come to you. If you decide to press a call bell, try doing that once. If no-one appears try again. Make sure you press it (call bell) once every minute unless if you are dying. Like I mentioned before, if it's a second drink you want, please don't even bother.

After the meal service a hot beverage is normally served. If you decide to order some always remember tea or coffee comes with milk/cream and sugar. If you don't take neither please make it known in time or you will irritate the guys serving you. Remember these guys are not your mothers. So do not expect them to guess if you take milk or sugar. Be smart jet-setter.

When you finish eating, don't try help pack your trays. The crew just hate being helped. The truth is you not helping at all by piling all the trash like an ancient man building pyramids or an Eiffel tower. All you will be doing is giving the poor soul extra work to rearrange your mess.

Also remember to say, 'thank you' after receiving or giving anything back to the person serving you. You don't have to but it's a good reflection on your mama. I m sorry but someone has to say it. Manners china, manners.

AFTER MEAL SERVICE

Most if not all international airlines sell articles on board on certain routes if time permits. Merchandise like jewelry, perfumes soveniours etc. If there is any flight crew that you wanted to charm,this is your chance. If you are American, European, Australian, South African or a New Zealander. This is your chance to flash your credit card. But if you are Chinese, Indian or Nigerian please use cash, chances are your credit card is fake (Just kidding). If you are north African, my brother oh, 'oga'(Nigerian for friend) ooh. Don't be shy my 'bruda'(Nigerian for brother) ooh, just show them the mooni (Nigerian for money). Trust me you might get lucky but don't hold me responsible if they (crew) just accept your stuff and give you a live morning news telephone number. Hey, why not take a risk, you are a jet-setter.

Remember when you stop crew members for these items make sure you buy something. There's no Victoria's Secrets moments on the jet where you just go window shopping and never buy. Crew don't have time to fulfill shopping fantasies. It's either you buy or keep your headphones on. There's no time for Mickey Mouse business on the airplane. No time for broke ass 'niggas' or cheap skates. Show them the dollar or turn a blind eye and zip it. You hear me? Inflight shopping doesn't take a lot of time, and when those carts are docked know that the main service is over.

LIGHTS OFF

Never try to chit chat crew after the onboard services since this is a special time for them to bond. Some become Dr Phil's of this world, marriage counsellors, or recruiters for drug peddling. You didn't hear it from me, but hey whatever the case might be this is not the right time to ask them the name of the river you flying over. Truthfully speaking there is no right time for such cheap talk. All you will get are names that do not exist. Names like 'Angazi' River. Thats isuZulu, in simple English it means 'no idea'.

Remember if money couldn't buy you love this might be the right time to faint. A crew member will definitely give you a kiss of life, but be warned they are a lot of gays and lesbians floating around. Your experience might not be as memorable as you intended it to be. You might be traumatized and need counseling after landing. If a medical emergency occurs and the crew call for a medical Doctor or practitioner, please don't come forward and try help to if you are a veterinary. Remember you do animals not human beings. Thank you anyway for your support but your hand is not required.

Always avoid use of sleeping tablets when you fly, you don't want the world to see how wide your mouth open, or best you can drool and snore in your sleep. Besides chances are you will wake up with a sore neck because of sleeping at the same position for long. If you want extra booze, say it straight. Don't come up with excuses like it helps you sleep. Trust me these guys have heard it all. Also avoid 'monkey see monkey do' kinda habits, they are annoying. Be original. Besides you came alone onto the jet so why get yourself into a drinking contest with the person next to you. If you decide not only to compete but become buddy jet-setters, please try keep it down when you converse. Remember you didn't hire a jet, all you did was book a seat.

If you are sitting next to a lady and it's a night flight then this might be your chance to try get lucky. No-one is in your way. Get her tiger, this could be an opportunity for you to join the mile high club. That's if she is a willing playmate. Just a high light from the jet-setter, you cannot join the mile high club alone. You definitely need a partner. If you wondering what the mile high club is all about, please ask someone sitting next to you. Like I said if you join the mile high club make sure the crew don't get to know of it or else they will spoil your fun. If you actually join this club make sure you have the right gear to play. We don't wanna come to your funeral a few months or years later.

HICK UPS

Oh yah before I forget, let me warn you. There are ups and downs of being a jet-setter depending on which part of the cabin you booked in. If you are traveling in 'cattle class' (coach/economy) gear yourself up for a cramped flight because most airlines don't give much leg room to the coach jet-setters but don't worry, you got me. A man with a million solutions to your problems. Super jet-setter. At this point in time you must stay focused don't rush things, relax china. If you don't want to sleep this is your chance to go to the kitchen and try chit chat the attendants. Choose wisely whom you gonna chat to and try to pick a subject that won't backfire. Try to talk about sports, it might work. Don't ever try to discuss politics, religion, gender or racial issues. You might scare off your prey. Be tactful when you talk about sports. Always try to gather as much info as possible before you announce a team you favor all else you might bruise nerves. Stay focused, remember the idea is not to outdo the person at your service but to buy time. Never suggest a drink whilst you are at it or else you will find your behind back in the cramped seat. Be as charming as a python Charlie, charming and goal oriented. Never loose focus. If you see nerves being touched. Loosen up and give in. Remember the idea is not to win. You just want to wile away time.

Never ask any flight crew if its possible for you to visit the flight deck because it's not allowed period. A free lesson from the jet-setter, all airlines don't allow any one into the cockpit inflight since 9/11. If you don't have a clue about 9/11 then like what the jet-setter always say, google it. All airlines don't trust anybody that is why they have adopted a closed door policy. I am not saying you are all terrorists, but hey you will back me up when I say prevention is better than cure. Who wants to end up in smoke. Maybe you do but obviously not me, the super jet-setter.

If you decide to sleep when the lights are off then this is your chance to slip behind the last row of seats. There's normally enough space for you to lay down. If you are brave you must look for a door written 'SILENCE PLEASE CREW AT REST' and slip in. I promise, you will find single beds in there. Discreetly choose one, close the curtain behind you and snore your way to your destination. But always remember not to get caught. If you do please don't blame me. All I m trying to do is help you live your dream in style. I know its hard like trying to drill a hole on a solid wall with a finger, but hey what's the heck. You are a jet-setter. If all your endeavors fail just walk around till the sun comes up. If you not flying into daylight just keep on walking till you hear the Adidas boys (Pilots) upfront talk about descent. Which ever side your dice fall on just know you have tried your best.

BREAKFAST

Whatever happened last night please don't take out your frustration on the super jet-setter. All I was trying to do is to help. Listen, don't be a sissy now and cry foul. Sh*t happens home boy. Get over it now and look forward to a brand new day. After all there is breakfast to look forward to. Once the lights are set to dim, know that breakfast is on its way. When the crew walk around the cabin soon after the lights come on please don't order anything. It's not yet time, it is preparation only. Flight crew will offer you hot towels to wipe drool of your faces. In case you don't know what I am talking about, a hot towel is a small piece of cloth/material big enough to wipe your face and hands clean enough to prepare you for your next feast. In simple words it's a wipe, the only difference is this one is hot.

Please do not try to wipe your armpits, ass or your sexual organs with it. It's not effective enough. Whatever you do please don't spit on it. I believe it will be dirty enough when you done with your quest for cleanliness. Damn, gross.

A few minutes after the towels you will see 'hosties' pushing carts towards you, I repeat do not order it's not yet time. The poor souls are trying to clean after your mess. As the crew gets to you please do not try to hand the dirty towel over to them. Simply throw them in the trash can they are pushing. Remember these guys have taken a lot of sh*t from you the whole flight and imagine how much they can still take. Don't take it personal I am being honest. Ok back to cleaning, please allow these guys to take care of you. Besides who wants to eat in a filthy environment? If you do, Lord have mercy. Unlike you some of us prefer otherwise. Getting rid of your dirt doesn't really take much time. Put your nostrils to work. I know you can smell it, breakfast is on it's way.

I understand some of you are royal and trust me this not the time to show off where come from. Don't expect pouched eggs or a descent bacon or some other fancy stuff your butler feeds you. What they have is what you'll get. Powdered eggs china. If there is a choice it might be cold meat and cheese which I always doubt it's freshness. Beside who promised you freshness, all you deserve is a stuffed tummy to help you conquer the traffic ahead of you. Like what the super jet-setter emphasizes, always take it like a man. Just a reminder, know how many sugars you take and always mention cream if you going to have some. Cream, milk. Same difference, it doesn't really matter to the jet-setter but just make sure you mention it.

Breakfast is bound to go quick, so in no time you should be stuffed up and ready to get off. After breakfast you might get documentation for your port of arrival. If you flying to the US and you happen to have received paperwork for customs and/or immigration please don't remind the flight attendants that you are American simply because it doesn't make a difference. Your uncle Obama wants you to do that paper work. Remember you are only American and not immune to formalities. If Australia is your final destination, brace yourself. Especially if you are black African. The immigration guys are waiting patiently to strip you naked. These eastern guys always come up with excuses of random checks. They will make you feel like a criminal. If you are very unfortunate they might stick their fingers up your ass. But hey what can I say, you are a jet-setter.

If you are flying domestic all you need to do is hold on, I don't want you vomiting all the goodies you had on landing. I m not saying you are going to puke but there is a huge possibility for new jet-setters.

Always keep your paper work with you. Do not try to give flight attendants your immigration form. Please use your brains. Customs forms, customs officers. Immigration forms, immigration officer. Repeat it loudly with me, immigration! Customs! You see it's simple.

On landing never clap your hands it simply shows how nervous you where throughout the flight. It's not a sin to be nervous but hey you don't want every Tom Dick and Harry to know your little secret. All you can do is hold on firmly to the armrests for safety. As the aircraft slows down on the runway please remain seated with your seat belt fastened until the plane comes to a complete stop and the captain switches off the seat belts lights then you may leave the aircraft. Always make sure that you have all your belongings with you. Whatever questions you might have for your final destination or connecting flight, please serve them for the ground staff. Aircrew has done their part and it is time for the jet-setters to get off and share their experiences with their hommies. Always remember that whatever experience you have had, it's always a pleasure for the super jet-setter to have you on board. And believe these guys when they say they look forward to seeing you again on one of their aircraft in the near future. Trust me they mean every word.

CONCLUSION

Being a jet-setter is not as complicated as rocket science. But to be a super jet-setter like me demands more. Super jet-setters are not a bunch of coffee 'moffies' or flying mattresses. Flight crew is highly trained, handpicked individuals who are experts in what they do. If you wanna be a super jet-setter all you got to do is always be situationally aware of your surroundings and remember not to check in your brains with your baggage. The super jet-setter has guided you enough for you to experience your moment of magic in style next time you decide to travel. It's up to you now to either take the advice or still maintain that I don't care attitude of yours. But always remember to give yourself a pat on the back for buying this handbook. You are the man. No,not me. You the main man. Adios amigos.

www.ingramcontent.com/pod-product-compliance
Lightning Source LLC
Chambersburg PA
CBHW020906310526
45786CB00018B/1856